Meetings that V.

Meetings that Work

KAREN E. SILVA

The Business Skills Express Series

BUSINESS ONE IRWIN/MIRROR PRESS
Burr Ridge, Illinois
New York, New York
Boston, Massachusetts

Mirror Press: David R. Helmstadter
                                 Carla F. Tishler

Editor-in-chief: Jeffrey A. Krames
Project editor: Stephanie M. Britt
Production manager: Diane Palmer
Interior designer: Jeanne M. Rivera
Art coordinator: Heather Burbridge
Illustrator: Boston Graphics, Inc.
Compositor: TCSystems, Inc.
Typeface: 12/14 Criterion
Printer: Malloy Lithographing, Inc.

Library of Congress Cataloging-in-Publication Data

Silva, Karen.
    Meetings that work / Karen E. Silva.
        p.   cm.—(Business skills express)
    ISBN 1-55623-866-5
    1. Meetings.   I. Title.   II. Series.
    HF5734.5.S57   1994
    658.4′56—dc20   93–18109

PREFACE

Have you ever thought, "I wish I could be more effective at meetings"? Or maybe you've envied other attendees' actions at meetings and wondered, "Why can't I do that?" Whatever your background experience or role at meetings—attending, conducting, or chairing—this book is designed to help you.

If you're relatively new in the business world and need some basic pointers, you'll find sound meeting principles outlined in this book. If you are experienced in business you'll find guidelines and insider suggestions to refresh your meeting skills. If you're chairing meetings, you'll find helpful tips and detailed checklists to make your next meeting more productive.

The best way to begin is by completing the Self-Assessment. This will help you assess your meeting skills. Next, work through each of the chapters at your own pace. Try to complete one chapter at each sitting so that you can focus completely on a single topic. Finally, take the Post-Test. As additional help, a Skill Maintenance checklist is included to measure your progress over the next months. You'll be pleased with the results and ongoing achievement.

Gook luck! You've begun your journey to improve your meeting skills.

Karen E. Silva

ABOUT THE AUTHOR

Karen E. Silva is Project Director and Associate Professor of Hospitality Management at Johnson and Wales University in Providence, R.I. She has extensive experience developing, teaching, and implementing comprehensive programs in hospitality and travel mangement for clients including Houghton Mifflin Company and Institute of Certified Travel Agents (ICTA). Karen Silva holds a Doctorate in Instructional Media and Technology.

ABOUT
BUSINESS ONE IRWIN

Business One Irwin is the nation's premier publisher of business books. As a Times Mirror company, we work closely with Times Mirror training organizations, including Zenger-Miller, Inc., Learning International, Inc., and Kaset International, to serve the training needs of business and industry.

About the Business Skills Express Series

This expanding series of authoritative, concise, and fast-paced books delivers high quality training on key business topics at a remarkably affordable cost. The series will help managers, supervisors, and front line personnel in organizations of all sizes and types hone their business skills while enhancing job performance and career satisfaction.

Business Skills Express books are ideal for employee seminars, independent self-study, on-the-job training, and classroom-based instruction. Express books are also convenient-to-use references at work.

CONTENTS

Self-Assessment   xiii

Chapter 1   1
Meetings, Meetings, Meetings
Meetings: They've Always Existed   1
Why Meet?   2
What Type of Meeting?   6
Focus on the Setting   6
Putting It Together   7

Chapter 2   9
Meeting Skills—The Basics
Successful and Not-So-Successful Meetings   9
Know What You Say without Words:
Nonverbal Communication   11
The Right Approach   12
Follow the Unwritten Rules   17
Putting It Together   19

Chapter 3   23
Meeting Skills—More Strategies
Who's in Charge?   23
Barriers and Problem Participants in Meetings   27
Meeting as Teambuilding   28
Follow-Up   32
Putting It Together   33

Chapter 4   37
Meeting Tools—The Extras
The Agenda   37
Meeting Plans   40
Audiovisual Equipment   41
Putting It Together   44

Post-Test   47

Suggested Solutions   51

Site Selection   53

Meetings Associations   57

Periodicals   59

Self-Assessment

How do you feel about your meeting skills? The Self-Assessment that follows may confirm your confidence or suggest areas for improvement. In either case, it will provide a starting point for you as you begin *Meetings that Work.*

	Almost always	Sometimes	Almost never
1. I feel confident at meetings.	_____	_____	_____
2. I know what type of meetings to plan, attend, or chair to accomplish my purpose.	_____	_____	_____
3. I possess the necessary skills to plan, conduct, or attend meetings.	_____	_____	_____
4. My nonverbal behavior sends the message I want during meetings.	_____	_____	_____
5. I am calm and objective at meetings.	_____	_____	_____
6. I am an effective listener.	_____	_____	_____
7. I use proper protocol when addressing others during meetings.	_____	_____	_____
8. I feel comfortable developing agendas.	_____	_____	_____
9. I effectively incorporate audiovisual equipment into my meeting presentations.	_____	_____	_____
10. I wish I could improve my meeting skills.	_____	_____	_____

Meetings, Meetings, Meetings

This chapter will help you to:

- Understand which types of meetings best suit specific purposes.
- Consider the issues of one-on-one meetings as well as group meetings.
- Consider the issues of meeting settings.

"So, what are you doing today?"

"Nothing much, just attending another meeting."

"Oh no, not another meeting!"

"Well, if I can just make it through this one, maybe I can get some *real* work done this week." ∎

If this sounds like a typical exchange, you're not alone. This book will: help you as a *participant* feel comfortable about attending meetings; help you as a *meeting planner* feel secure in your organizational skills; and help you as a meeting *chairperson* feel confident in your decision-making and leadership skills. You and your team members will be able to limit time spent in unproductive meetings by making your meetings more productive.

MEETINGS: THEY'VE ALWAYS EXISTED

Since the beginning of time, people have gathered for meetings of one sort or another, whether as clans of cavemen joining together to hunt game, Alexander the Great meeting with his generals to plan strategy, or the knights of King Arthur jousting and crusading during meetings at the round table.

Nearly everyone in his or her career attends meetings. The typical supervisor spends on an average more than 25 percent of his or her time in meetings. Mid- and upper-level management often devote more than 40 percent of their time to meetings. Some of these meetings may be informal sessions near the watercooler or coffee maker, while others may be week-long sessions at faraway destinations. Many meetings are held in-house in boardrooms, conference rooms, or private offices. Others are held in conference centers far from the office.

Look through local newspapers to see what kinds of seminars or other types of meetings are being advertised in your field.

WHY MEET?

Meeting purposes are as varied as the locations and the participants. Some sessions are corporate-sponsored annual events, others are devoted to developing new skills, while still others are for decision-making or information-gathering.

Common Reasons for Holding Meetings

- To exchange or provide information.
- To make better informed decisions.
- To brainstorm.
- To establish goals or objectives.
- To delegate tasks or authority.
- To share responsibility for a project.
- To persuade others.
- To motivate or inspire.
- To monitor relationships.
- To provide a social outlet.
- To advise and counsel.

No matter what the purpose, successful meetings rely on planning, organization, and follow-through by the attendees, the planner, and the leader.

Who is responsible for planning meetings in your organization?_____

_____

_____

WHAT TYPE OF MEETING?

Depending on purpose, there are many different types of meetings.

Read through these descriptions and note the types of meetings you have been asked to: attend (A), organize (O), or conduct (C). Has it always been clear *why* the particular type was chosen?

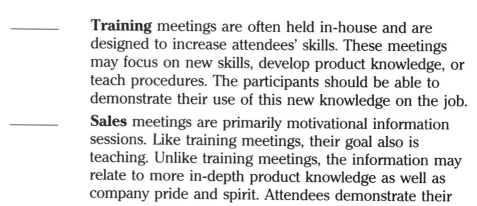

_____   **Training** meetings are often held in-house and are designed to increase attendees' skills. These meetings may focus on new skills, develop product knowledge, or teach procedures. The participants should be able to demonstrate their use of this new knowledge on the job.

_____   **Sales** meetings are primarily motivational information sessions. Like training meetings, their goal also is teaching. Unlike training meetings, the information may relate to more in-depth product knowledge as well as company pride and spirit. Attendees demonstrate their

1

use of this information through increased sales figures and stronger morale.

_____ Senior **executive** meetings are usually for high-ranking corporate officials such as CEOs, directors, presidents, or vice presidents. These meetings typically provide information about profitability, planning and strategy, long-term goals, and pivotal leadership issues. Though often relatively small in size, these sessions need to be very smoothly run and highly professional.

_____ **Informational seminars** can be large or small in size, depending on the topic and the needs of the organization. The program is usually presented by an expert in the field or a panel made up of knowledgeable members. Frequently, speakers provide preprinted information to attendees for study prior to the seminar, or as reference material for follow-up activities.

_____ **Committee/team** meetings are held as the need arises. Participants are expected to bring equal levels of commitment and enthusiasm to share with group members. Such meetings are frequently project-based and require differing lengths of time and levels of dedication, depending on the complexity of the project.

_____ **Departmental** meetings are functional sessions that provide timely information to department members. Often headed by a department manager, these meetings are typically scheduled on a weekly or monthly rotating basis.

_____ **Conventions** that are held off-site provide the stereotypical image of what large meetings are supposed to be. Such sessions may range from one or two days to one or two weeks. Conventions often include numerous social functions and related activities such as tours. A trade show can be considered a type of convention that offers a variety of expert speakers, displays, and exhibits. Conventions frequently necessitate overnight accommodations and transportation arrangements. These are expensive investments for any organization.

_____ **Crisis meetings** are held if there are delays in product development or changes in competitive advertising occur. Executives may call special crisis meetings to discuss strategy. These are typically relatively short but are tightly focused and results-oriented.

———   **Meal-time meetings** take place when time is money, participants want to receive the best value for their dollar, and use their time efficiently. For this reason, many meetings are held during breakfast, lunch, or dinner.

Coffee breaks are perhaps the most common form of food and beverage service at meetings. When planning coffee breaks, a primary concern is interruption of the meeting. Ideally, coffee should be set up in an adjacent room or break-out area. If this is not feasible, a coffee setup in the room prior to the beginning of the meeting will add to the general hospitality. Later, refreshments can be added at an agreed on time to coincide with a break in the meeting's agenda. *Usually one to two hours is a good guideline for replenishing food and beverage.*

■   T i p s ——————————————————————

With today's increasing emphasis on health, many participants are looking for a change in the traditional coffee and donut fare. For a comparable price, items such as juice, yogurt, and fresh fruit can be substituted. Brewed decaf coffee and specialty teas also provide a diversion. Afternoon breaks might include similar items, bottled water or seltzers, or even vegetable dips or cheese platters instead of cookies and desserts.

If you are planning or conducting a meeting, of course you need to know what kind of meeting suits the purposes for getting people together.

If you are a participant, you need to know the difference between types of meetings to better understand your role and level of involvement, and to better achieve your organization's expectations. No one wants to attend an informal outdoor function while dressed in boardroom attire. Conversely, you certainly wouldn't want to be the featured speaker for a companywide formal seminar when you only anticipate a hands-on team workshop. Your understanding of the purpose and nature of the meeting must be clear so that you and your organization can get the most from it.

Your Place or Mine?

You probably participate in one-on-one meetings every day. How many times do you find yourself setting up a meeting with just one colleague to cover an issue? Although these aren't formal meetings where participants sit around a table and move through an agenda, one-on-one meetings are where much of day-to-day business takes place. Like all meetings there is an unspoken protocol:

- Holding a meeting in your own office allows the greatest degree of control. You're on home turf and can set the direction of the meeting.

- The person of the higher rank should decide the location. Usually, this person holds the meeting in his or her office.

- Remaining standing during the meeting will promote a sense of confidence and authority.

- Desks are often used as natural barriers. Watch the body language of the other participant to see if he or she seems accommodating to your ideas, or blocked against them. Sitting at the same side of the desk or at an adjacent table sends a message that participants will work as a team.

- Share coffee or a snack with your colleague. This sends a message that comradery is valued and problem solving will occur in a hospitable setting.

FOCUS ON THE SETTING

The environment of the meeting room can also have a great impact on a meeting. As you begin to think about setting up your meeting, consider the following issues as you evaluate the suitability of your meeting space:

1

- Temperature setting is comfortable and can be regulated.
- Noise level is conducive to a productive meeting.
- Meeting space is away from distractions.
- Telephone interruptions can be limited.
- Seating space is adequate.
- Round tables are available for discussions.
- Lighting is adequate.
- Audiovisual equipment is available.
- Internal distractions are limited (windows, heating/cooling system noises, or clutter).
- Bathroom facilities are nearby.

PUTTING IT TOGETHER

Meetings come in all shapes and sizes. Yet, whatever the location, length, or level of formality, each meeting has its own purpose. To be successful, meetings must provide a common ground for effective communication.

Planners often find that the procedures for developing different types of successful meetings are quite similar. Just as planners become more comfortable with increased experience, so do meeting leaders. Participants also become more familiar with types and purposes of meetings based on frequent attendance.

Review & Practice

List the types of meetings your group holds.

_____

_____

_____

Briefly note the main reasons meetings play an important role in your job.

_____

_____

_____

Chapter Checkpoints

✓ The formal meeting planning process is relatively recent.

✓ Nearly everyone attends meetings.

✓ Keep in mind that one-on-one meetings are a good place to get work done—be prepared for them.

✓ Make sure meeting rooms are appropriately set up, and conducive to productive discussion.

2 | Meeting Skills— The Basics

This chapter will help you to:

- Identify successful meeting skills.
- Develop effective nonverbal communication skills.
- Evaluate the importance of listening.
- Develop appropriate meeting attitudes.
- Practice greeting protocol.
- Consider valid reasons for not attending meetings.

SUCCESSFUL AND NOT-SO-SUCCESSFUL MEETINGS

Successful meetings achieve a common goal through communication and collective action. They leave everyone feeling positive, motivated, and productive.

Some planners, chairpersons, and participants believe that there's a secret formula for successful meetings. Since meetings are high profile events in which you could be judged by others, people must discover their own secrets to gain the most from every meeting.

Unfortunately, not every meeting is a success. How often have you attended a meeting that is boring? Or too lengthy? Or very disorganized? Even worse, mediocre meeting style can be contagious—one bad meeting can set the tone for the rest of the day, the week, and for future meetings. In fact, meeting experts claim that nearly 50 percent of all business meetings are inefficient. Frequently this is due to lack of planning or follow through by the meeting planner.

Whatever the reason, a bad meeting spells lost opportunity for the organizer and the participants. In today's information-based, service-oriented society, the increasing importance of interpersonal communication is nowhere better demonstrated than in a meeting. Careers can be jeopardized or advanced when supervisors evaluate the skills of participants during a meeting.

Check off the skills necessary to successfully plan (P), attend (A), and conduct (C) meetings:

_____	Organizational skills.
_____	Flexibility.
_____	Creativity.
_____	Sense of humor.
_____	Follow through.
_____	Attention to detail.
_____	Recordkeeping.
_____	Listening skills.
_____	Time management.

List other skills you believe are necessary to successfully plan (P) meetings:

_____
_____
_____

What skills are helpful when attending (A) meetings?

_____
_____
_____

What skills are vital when conducting (C) a meeting?

_____
_____
_____

Which of these skills do you need to improve to be more effective in meetings? How can you develop these skills? Who could help mentor you or evaluate your progress?

_____
_____
_____
_____

KNOW WHAT YOU SAY WITHOUT WORDS: NONVERBAL COMMUNICATION

2

It is important to be aware of the signals we send in meetings since signals sent through nonverbal behavior account for approximately 55 percent of what we communicate. These signals include facial expression, eye contact, distance, posture, use of hands, arms, legs, and other body movement. We may send messages that we don't intend to, especially during the initial minutes of a meeting.

Which of these common meeting behaviors are positive (P) examples of nonverbal communication? Which are negative (N) examples?

_____	• Yawning
_____	• Tapping pencil/pen
_____	• Eye contact
_____	• Doodling
_____	• Weak handshake
_____	• Leaning forward
_____	• Nodding
_____	• Crossed arms
_____	• Crossed legs
_____	• Smiling
_____	• Interrupting

Can some of these be both positive and negative?

Tone of voice and other such cues can also reveal a great deal about our feelings during meetings. How long we speak, how frequently we repeat words or phrases, our fluency of speech, and the pitch of our voice will tell others more than we might believe.

Rate yourself:

Y N   Do you use reinforcers when you speak? (Okay, um hum, ah, or um.)

Y N   Do you enunciate clearly?

Y N   Do you speak at a comfortable speed for listeners?

Y N   Is the volume of your voice appropriate?

Y N   Is your voice pleasant, with a variable pitch and upbeat, positive tone?

Y N   Do you sound self-assured?

Tips ————————————————————————

For better nonverbal communication in meetings:

1. In face-to-face conversation, maintain eye contact 90 percent of the time.

2. If standing, evenly distribute your weight on both feet.

3. When sitting, maintain a straight posture, leaning forward slightly.

4. Use open-handed gestures to demonstrate key points.

5. Maintain a distance of two to four feet for business communication, less distance for intimate conversations, and more distance for public interactions.

6. Nod your head to acknowledge understanding.

7. Stand up when you are introduced.

During your next department meeting, observe the nonverbal cues of the participants. What hadn't you noticed before? What unspoken messages are really being sent?

_____

_____

THE RIGHT APPROACH

A good approach to nonverbal behavior is simply to start with the right attitude. You can actually begin much earlier than the meeting itself. Deciding on the right clothing and arriving on time are two examples of getting into a positive mode of nonverbal communication.

Tips ————————————————————————

A good appearance will improve your confidence, which will contribute to your overall success at meetings.

Arrive Early

Arrive early at a meeting, especially if you are the planner or chairperson.

2

Attendees should arrive a few minutes early to mingle with coworkers, especially if refreshments are being served. Many times informal networking sessions develop prior to the actual meeting. Prompt arrival also indicates a sincere interest in the upcoming proceedings, while late arrival sends a clear message of disregard for the presenter, agenda, and participants.

Choose the Right Seat

Choosing the correct seat can send a strong nonverbal message. Unless round tables are used, the leader of the meeting should always sit at the head of a table or near the podium—a prime way to indicate who is in charge. Other key attendees should usually sit near the leader.

Participants should also select their seats carefully. Some seats are poor choices due to viewing or hearing difficulties. Food and audiovisual equipment can also be a consideration in seat selection. No one wants to hear the buzz of the overhead projector's fan. Planners should be tuned in to the needs of each attendee when choosing the best possible room setup for the meeting.

In general, semicircles present the best opportunity for communication. Face-to-face seating, as at long tables, provides control but can also trigger or intensify confrontation. For this reason, in formal meetings, it is advisable to assign seats. This is particularly important if potential adversaries will be attending the same session.

If informal meetings occur routinely, traditional seating, where members sit in "ordained" chairs, may be the norm. Some of the most common seating arrangements are shown in the figures on page 14.

Observe your next department meeting. Where did the leader sit? Where did other key participants sit? Try this exercise. Look at the sample seating arrangements. Which seats would be best for maximum exposure and control of the meeting's discussion? Which would be the worst?

Conference styles

Board of directors: No podium/stage/dais or head table

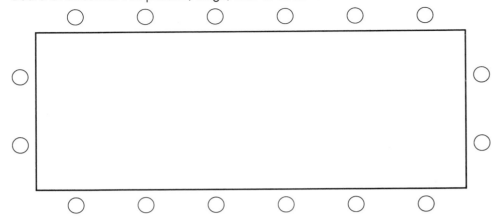

Rounds: Often used for group discussions, workshops, or food functions

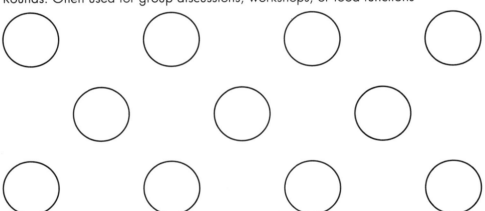

U-shaped: Variations can be an "E" or a "T"

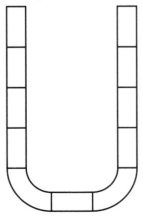

Listen Attentively

Good listeners often control discussions. Why? Perhaps because, as studies have shown, an average listener only pays attention to 25 percent of what is said. Most listeners can comprehend 500 or more words per minute, yet most speakers talk at a rate of 125 to 250 words per minute. *Concentration* is the key to effective active listening.

When listening during meetings, try these techniques:

Try to predict what speakers will say.

Review what has already been discussed.

Clarify ambiguous points in your own mind.

Listen for meaning and feeling, not just words.

Take notes.

Ask pertinent questions to direct the discussion.

Focus on understanding, not on distractions.

Put In Your Two Cent's Worth

Just as it is important to listen carefully at meetings, it is equally important to contribute to them. Each person should plan to contribute something of value. Every person can make a unique contribution. Show a positive and supportive attitude in your verbal and nonverbal behavior.

As a participant, you must contribute pertinent information if an issue is raised that affects your department, job, staff, and so forth. Studies have shown that individuals who are willing to introduce issues early in a meeting will have a better chance of exerting influence later. Be sure to state your ideas clearly and concisely.

Hints

A handy formula to remember is:
STATE your point succinctly,
SUPPORT and explain your point,
SUMMARIZE your original point.

When You Disagree

If you make a point that is in basic conflict with others, be sure to agree with those facts that you can, then state your disagreement with those you can't, using adequate support.

Finally, summarize your argument. In this way you demonstrate a positive willingness to work as a team, your superior listening skills, and your ability to assimilate information and draw conclusions.

If debate becomes heated, know when to hold your ground, and most important, when to relinquish it gracefully. Some hints for disagreeing:

Consider posing your ideas as a suggestion, not an ultimatum.

Ask questions that will lead to conclusions.

Volunteer to follow up.

Inform your supervisor of all important decisions and actions.

Think of the last time you disagreed with someone at a meeting. How did you communicate your disagreement? How might you have communicated your disagreement differently and more effectively?

_____

_____

_____

Prepare Carefully

If you are planning or running a meeting you can't be too prepared. For successful meetings, be sure to:

Before the Meeting	At the Meeting
■ Set expectations high	■ Be specific in what you want to accomplish
■ Use committees to help organize and coordinate	■ Maintain goals and objectives despite distractions
■ Announce meeting times well in advance	■ Don't waste time on irrelevant issues
■ Distribute the agenda in advance and follow it	■ Minimize interruptions
■ Observe the time constraints	
■ List agenda items in order of priority	

2

Body Language Speaks a Thousand Words

Jeff was a newly hired legal assistant. One of his first tasks was to attend the weekly departmental meeting held in the main office. Wanting to make a good impression, he arrived early and placed his briefcase on a chair near the head of the table. He then left the room to make a quick call. When he returned he fixed a cup of coffee and returned to his seat.

During the meeting Jeff felt he was being watched, so he contributed as frequently as possible. This made him very nervous, so he drank a great deal of water and refilled his coffee cup frequently. He also doodled on his notes so that others would think he was paying attention. When the chairperson asked a question Jeff smiled and nodded in agreement. About halfway through the meeting, Jeff's secretary interupted the session to inform him that he had a visitor. Upon his return, twenty minutes later, Jeff asked the person next to him what had happened.

After the meeting he hurried back to his desk to begin all of the work that had been waiting. Later that day his supervisor asked him to summarize the meeting. ■

In the space below, comment on ways Jeff could have controlled his nonverbal behavior and increased his concentration.

_____

_____

_____

_____

_____

(See page 51 for a suggested solution.)

FOLLOW THE UNWRITTEN RULES

Volumes could be written on the importance of company rules, customs, or protocol—meeting etiquette. It may not be necessary to consult the procedures bible, Robert's Rules of Order, but certain customs, traditions, and common courtesy should be observed to ensure successful meetings. After all, as with any successful team, you need to know the rules to be able to play the game well.

What's in a Name?

Universal rules govern the use of names and entertainment style at the typical business luncheon or today's more popular "power breakfast." For example, what title would you use in a meeting when referring to your supervisor? To your secretary? To your peers? To your staff?

- If in doubt, use title and surname at formal meetings.
- Introductions often indicate status in a company.
- Take your cue from others at informal meetings or simply ask about the usual style of addressing participants.

Let's Do Lunch

Who picks up the check?

- Simply stated, the person who invites others to a luncheon, dinner, or breakfast meeting usually pays the check. If in doubt, you can always offer to pay, even if you are the invitee. Most often, the higher-ranking member will volunteer to pay.
- Protocol relating to ordering meals and drinks should also be handled by the person who will be paying the bill.
- Be sure to reply promptly to invitations.
- As with all business meetings, know when and where the meeting will be held and what its purpose is.

Imagine that you are going to organize a breakfast, luncheon, or dinner meeting to discuss an important business issue. Consider who to invite, where and when the meeting will be held, and what the agenda might be. Would this meeting be more successful at a particular time of day? Who should pay the bill?

_____

_____

_____

_____

_____

_____

_____

May I Be Excused?

Sometimes, as a participant, you may wish to be excused from a meeting. There are many legitimate reasons for being excused. Perhaps the meeting interferes with your preexisting schedule. You may feel nothing will be accomplished and it will be a waste of your time. This is a delicate situation and requires diplomacy on your part. Some strategies include:

- Simply question whether your attendance is required.
- State your reason for wanting to be excused.
- Reaffirm that you have a scheduling conflict and will not be available.
- Ask another participant to respond for you and clarify details.
- Just say no.

Some of these strategies are easier said than done, but with practice and good judgment you will be able to control the number of meetings you must attend.

Recall the last time you wanted to be excused from a meeting. How did you handle it? How might you have handled it better?

_____

_____

_____

_____

PUTTING IT TOGETHER

The secret to successful meetings really is no mystery. It is a carefully planned and executed series of learned behaviors, common sense, and judgment.

■ Review & Practice

Consider the last unsuccessful meeting that you attended. What went wrong? How could problems have been avoided? _____

_____

_____

_____

List two nonverbal behaviors that you want to improve. _____

_____

_____

_____

_____

_____

Discuss how the right attitude affects punctuality, participation, and listening. _____

_____

_____

Chapter Checkpoints

✓ Interpersonal communication skills are vitally important in meetings.

✓ Meetings often take much longer to plan than to hold.

✓ Signals sent through nonverbal behavior account for approximately 55 percent of communication.

✓ Clothing can be an important nonverbal cue.

✓ No matter what your position, early arrival at a meeting indicates interest.

✓ Most listeners only pay attention to one quarter of what is said.

✓ It is important to contribute at meetings.

✓ Knowing when and how to disagree is an important meeting skill.

✓ Protocol and etiquette are key factors in meetings.

3 | Meeting Skills— More Strategies

This chapter will help you to:

- Learn strategies for meetings with subordinates, peers, and superiors.
- Consider ways to deal with barriers and problem participants in meetings.
- View meetings as teambuilding.
- Learn effective decision-making steps for meetings.

The individual who runs the meeting is most responsible for its success or failure. Participants who wish to get the most out of a meeting also need to make preparations. Establishing a sense of teamwork and responsibility saves time and effort and helps to achieve everyone's objectives.

WHO'S IN CHARGE?

As a meeting leader you have a twofold task: to get work done and to establish teambuilding.

Meeting with subordinates is perhaps the least complex situation if you are the leader. In this case you have implied power and authority. This can backfire, however, because subordinates may not feel comfortable providing candid feedback during discussions. Some strategies to ensure productive meetings with subordinates include:

- Outlining your objectives clearly.
- Setting clear parameters for discussion.
- Encouraging democratic participation.
- Seeking effective solutions.

- Reserving judgment and opinion.
- Delegating and sharing responsibility.

Meeting with peers is quite a different situation. Control is not clearly established and natural competition may result. Participants may question your authority and challenge your plans with their own agendas. To meet more effectively with peers:

- Use humor and past shared experiences.
- Begin with a formal agenda, then move to the informal.
- Consult with peers prior to the meeting.
- Obtain authority from a higher level, and mention this during the meeting.

Meeting with superiors can also provide a challenge. In this case, even though you are the leader you may feel intimidated or just plain nervous. The important point to remember is that you offer special expertise that is respected and needed in this particular situation. When leading superiors:

- Present your case clearly, then propose your solution.
- Ask for action and commitment.
- Remember that you are a resource of knowledge and information to the others.
- Don't waste time.
- Don't aggressively challenge their authority.

Providing Leadership

Whatever group you lead, you have the responsibility to provide vision and leadership. Participants will look to you to control unruly members, encourage and protect reluctant members, and, above all, remain impartial. (Having been chosen as the leader, you, of course, have the wisdom, flexibility, and communication and interpersonal skills to influence others to achieve your objectives!) In general, if you do your homework and get others to do theirs, you will be more successful. Some general suggestions for the leader:

- Limit the number of participants and issues.
- Unite the group by defining roles.

- State and restate your purpose periodically.
- Seek, clarify, and reflect the ideas of others.
- Control emotions.
- Don't draw attention to specific members (e.g., latecomers).
- Move the meeting along at a steady, step-by-step pace.
- Begin and end on time.

3

If you can convince everyone to contribute and participate, they will be more motivated and committed to the outcomes of the meeting. In short, a united, focused group will be easier to mobilize.

Tips

Have you ever tried any of these motivating tips?

_____ Send colorful, unique meeting notices rather than memos.

_____ Begin meetings with some sort of icebreaker or game.

_____ Start meetings with a task or activity that requires physical movement.

_____ Use background music as attendees arrive to create ambiance.

_____ Greet participants with a smile and handshake.

_____ Ask group members to introduce others.

_____ Start with a funny story or tasteful joke.

Use one of these ideas to create your own unique opener for your next meeting.

Leadership Styles: Choose One that Works

National Cargo's branch office is run by a motivated, enthusiastic, take-charge leader. Every Monday morning he calls his managerial staff together for a half-hour session to focus on weekly priorities. At the end of this meeting, managers feel positive and energized and share this productive energy with their departments.

The company is so pleased with this leader that they have promoted him to a position in the corporate office. His replacement was a detail-oriented person who had been loyal to the company for many years. Hearing about the success of the Monday morning sessions, he decided to continue the tradition. However, the new manager only focused on details of everyone's work, and questioned many of their decisions. Consequently, the former half-hour pep sessions soon became lengthy diatribes. Members began to resent the time taken from their work and became sullen, despondent, and inattentive. The quality of work from the departments and staff suffered. ■

What changes need to be made to get these sessions back on track?

_____

_____

_____

_____

(See page 51 for a suggested solution.)

Smoking Policies

Whatever the size of the meeting, the smoking policy will be an issue. The best way to handle this problem is to consider it prior to the meeting. How large or small is the meeting room? What is the setup of the room? What is the company's or the state's policies on smoking? Is the ventilation in the room adequate? How many people in the group smoke? Can the needs of both groups be accommodated?

An effective way to deal with this problem is to arrange for a nonsmoking room and limit smoking to coffee breaks. If the room is large enough to divide and the ventilation system is adequate, the group can be split into smokers and nonsmokers. Of course, if your meeting is held in a state with clean air legislation, such as Minnesota, smoking in public will not be an issue. Smoking can be a sensitive subject, depending on the size and nature of the group, and it should be addressed by the meeting planner well in advance.

View Meetings as Teams

Each group that meets is like a team that goes through the usual stages of team development: forming, storming, norming, and conforming. During the forming stage, group members are polite, introducing themselves and their ideas. Storming follows, as each member freely discusses and promotes his or her point of view. Norming will signal the beginning of group agreement. Finally, conforming will lead to group acceptance of certain proposals. The more quickly you can move to consensus in the final stage, the more successful your meeting will be.

Remember that consensus differs from compromise. Consensus indicates that each member feels comfortable with his or her contribution and the final decision. Groups that compromise are frequently dissatisfied with both the process and the outcome because many feel they have given in to others' wishes rather than being true to their own beliefs. In general, groups that reach consensus are more positive, motivated, and satisfied with the decision-making process than groups that merely agree to disagree.

3

BARRIERS AND PROBLEM PARTICIPANTS IN MEETINGS

No matter how carefully you plan or how closely you follow sound guidelines, you may still encounter problems with participants. We assume that people meet because they share common purposes or interests. Once together, even the most logical individuals sometimes place personal priorities ahead of the overall objectives of the meeting. Otherwise competent, rational individuals seem to replay the roles of Dr. Jeckyll and Mr. Hyde.

Participants sometimes come to the meeting with their own personal agendas. Perhaps they are motivated by blind ambition or thirst for power. Others may be filled with insecurities and personal feelings and emotions. Some may view the meeting as a great substitute for working—a way to escape daily pressures. Still others may attend because they have been told to or because it is viewed as the thing to do. Social participants often use meetings as a time to broaden their social contacts. As a leader you need to understand these barriers, recognize your allies, and control your challengers for the good of the entire group.

Review and label the following list of behavior characteristics. Some members will display supportive (S) traits, while others will be disruptive (D).

_____	Initiating.	_____	Criticizing.
_____	Supportive.	_____	Attention seeking.
_____	Blocking.	_____	Disinterested.
_____	Cynical.	_____	Manipulative.
_____	Aggressive.	_____	Miscommunicating.
_____	Reconciling.	_____	Distracting, rambling.
_____	Egotistical.	_____	Incompetent.
_____	Contributing.	_____	Sharing responsibility.
_____	Refocusing.	_____	Sharing risk.
_____	Clarifying.	_____	Silent.
_____	Facilitating.		

Have you ever been at a meeting and observed some of these undesirable characteristics in participants? How did the leader handle these individuals? How did the leader reward members exhibiting supportive traits?

_____

_____

_____

MEETING AS TEAMBUILDING

As the leader of the meeting, you must motivate each group member to actively participate and contribute. In this way, members will be committed to the final decisions that are reached. How can you engage everyone's participation? If you, as the leader, view the meeting as a teambuilding process, you'll have a framework for making decisions and reaching consensus.

Stage One—Planning, Forming, or Setting the Ground Rules

In the first stage of teambuilding in a meeting, you'll create common ground, gather facts, make inferences, and define the problem.

Provide a brief history or background of the topics under discussion. This lays common groundwork for what will follow. It also ensures that everyone at the meeting is working from the same shared base of knowledge.

Provide facts about the topics under discussion. Listing these again (perhaps in outline form on a handout or on an overhead) stimulates cohesion and provides common information.

Suggest a set of inferences from the facts. This is a crucial area because some members may try to provide assumptions rather than inferences based on *facts*. These inferences can later be used for discussion purposes.

Define the problem or topic under discussion. It helps to be as clear as possible so that members don't concentrate on extraneous details rather than the actual problem.

One of the biggest threats to a meeting arises when participants don't act as if they are on the same team. Some disagreement is inevitable and healthy but it is important to dispel aggressive behavior as quickly as possible and to unite the team.

Stage Two—Organizing the Team, Storming, or Running the Race

In the second stage of teambuilding, encourage members to express feelings, make contributions, avoid blame, get the facts, and brainstorm.

Allow members to express their feelings. Often if a point of contention is brought up before a group, all members with the concern will be more receptive to reason and facts.

3

Acknowledge team members for their contributions.   Doing so has a positive effect on the whole group.

Avoid taking sides or allocating blame once discussion begins.   Remaining calm and defusing tension through humor can be constructive tactics.

Reiterate facts, not opinions.   To lessen tension, ask specific questions that require factual information, not value judgments.

Brainstorm to develop a list of alternative solutions to the problem.   Brainstorming is helpful for discussion and problem solving. Remember, brainstorming allows for the free flow of ideas from all participants no matter how obscure these ideas may seem to be at the time. Don't evaluate ideas until they're all on the table. Great solutions often come from brainstorming.

Once conflict is eliminated, it is vital to focus the team on its specific agenda. Some participants may sidetrack others or go off on tangents that will not be constructive for the group. New conflicts may arise as participants refocus on their own agendas. A minor diversion is fine, particularly if the discussion has been intense, but it's important to get back to the topic at hand as quickly as possible so that momentum is not lost.

Stage Three—Leading, Norming, or the Finish Line Is in Sight

In the third stage of teambuilding in a meeting, decision making moves toward consensus. At this stage it is crucial to listen, watch nonverbal behavior, and focus on understanding.

Actively listen to the discussion at hand.   Effective listeners take notes, ask pertinent questions, paraphrase, and summarize key points.

Use nonverbal cues such as eye contact, clearing your throat, or tapping a pencil to interrupt when rambling occurs.   If this is too indirect, make an actual comment to the effect that the conversation is getting off track.

Check for understanding.   If a point seems to be irrelevant, ask for clarification as to the relationship of this point to the discussion.

Check for accuracy.   Recapping will be useful for all participants and ensures that everyone shares an understanding of key points.

Consider the pros (benefits) and cons (disadvantages) of each possible solution.   Many of the solutions may revolve around the issues of time, effort, money, and human resources.

Through consensus, choose the best possible solution.   Review all members' input and discuss which option provides the best solution—get everyone involved.

At this juncture, conflict and meandering are controlled, and the team's real work can begin. Mobilizing the team to take action involves a series of decision-making steps. Often, participants become eager to settle a problem without considering all of the possible alternatives.

Stage Four—Controlling, Conforming, or Crossing the Finish Line

In the fourth stage of teambuilding in a meeting, focus on reaching consensus and deciding how to implement it. The leader's role is to control and encourage discussion, take notes, maintain positive attitudes, and make implementation plans.

Control dominant personalities and encourage timid individuals.   Suggest that no one interrupts another team member, and elicit contributions from quieter members through probing questions. If aggression begins, suggest a private discussion after the meeting.

Encourage all participants to contribute.   The ideas of each member, as an integral part of the team, are important to its success.

Take notes.   Ideally, a flipchart or overhead projector can be used to record information so that everyone can see the group's progress. Recording everyone's contributions may spark further discussion and also encourage participation.

Promote a positive mental attitude.   Ensure that the group is involved and committed to reaching the best solution—let members know that they are vital to the success of the problem-solving process.

3

Develop a plan for effective implementation. Determine who will be responsible for each step of the follow-up process.

Think of a meeting that would have benefited from this four-stage strategy. How could you use the four teambuilding stages in that example or during your last meeting?

_____

_____

_____

_____

_____

_____

_____

FOLLOW-UP

No meeting is really complete without some form of follow-up. Often, meetings require written minutes that are forwarded to all attendees and supervisors. Many leaders request written evaluations of meetings to provide quantitative data for future meetings. Detailed reports may even be necessary. Those responsible for written materials need to be especially attentive when taking notes or recording information to follow up. The leader is responsible for delegating these tasks.

A simple follow-up record could include:

- The time, date, location of the meeting, and attendees.
- The time the meeting ended.
- All agenda items and decisions.
- The names of those responsible for follow-up action.
- The major suggestions and relevant points.
- The pertinent information relating to the next meeting.

Evaluating Your Meeting

Consider how you _want_ a meeting to be conducted, then compare the actual minutes and results of the same meeting. Did the real meeting meet your expectations? Did it follow a plan and reach a constructive conclusion?

Review the following guidelines on meeting effectiveness.

Y   N   Did I need this meeting?

Y   N   Did it preclude other more important meetings?

Y   N   Did I have goals and objectives and did I accomplish them?

Y   N   Were the group members aware of these goals and objectives?

Y   N   Did I have the authority and responsibility to be the leader?

Y   N   Was I adequately prepared?

Y   N   Did the right people attend?

Y   N   If I ran this meeting again, would I do it differently?

Y   N   Was this the best possible use of everyone's time and effort?

PUTTING IT TOGETHER

Strategies differ for every meeting.

Contribution is a key factor whether you are the planner, participant, or chairperson, although attendees may bring their own personal agendas. Leaders must actively control the proceedings and use teambuilding skills to reach consensus.

■ Review & Practice

When was your last meeting with subordinates? Peers? Superiors? What worked and what didn't? How could you improve a meeting next time?

_____
_____
_____
_____

What motivating tips can you offer for beginning and ending your meetings?

_____
_____
_____

Have you ever dealt with smoking as an issue at one of your meetings? If so, what strategies did you use successfully?

_____

_____

How could you integrate the four stages of teambuilding into your next meeting?

_____

_____

_____

_____

Chapter Checkpoints

✓ Meetings with subordinates, peers, and superiors all have their own unique characteristics and strategies.

✓ A leader's role includes providing vision, controlling, encouraging, protecting, and remaining impartial.

✓ First impressions are vital to pique participants' interest.

✓ Meetings are ideal opportunities for teambuilding.

✓ Attendees come to meetings with their own personal agendas that may or may not be in the best interests of the team.

✓ A four-step teambuilding approach is one of the most effective methods of problem solving.

4 | Meeting Tools—The Extras

This chapter will help you to:

- Design an effective agenda.
- Distinguish between an agenda and a meeting plan.
- Review the best uses of audiovisual equipment.

Planners, leaders, and attendees require a variety of tools to make meetings effective. These important tools can make or break a meeting.

THE AGENDA

Handouts of printed materials are vital meeting tools. As with all visual aids, success depends on quality, brevity, and creativity. Perhaps the most important of these written items is the agenda. When properly constructed, the agenda can be the key to organization, communication, control, and success.

Distribute an agenda prior to the actual meeting so that participants can prepare for the topics that will be discussed. But don't distribute the agenda so far in advance that participants have the opportunity to misplace or forget it. Usually, a two-day lead time is sufficient for routine meetings. An additional day may be necessary for larger or more complex meetings. Due to their very nature, crisis meetings are the exception, where brief agendas may be handed out during the meeting.

A one- or two-page agenda for a meeting should always include:

- Date of meeting.
- Time of meeting.
- Location of meeting.

- Contact person and telephone number.
- Topics to be discussed.
- Suggested time schedule for each topic.
- Names of participants reporting on topics.

If you are participating in a meeting, try to make sure that your topic gets a priority position on the agenda. Those topics given the most weight and consideration are usually addressed at the beginning of the session. If you anticipate trouble you may want to place your item near the end when less discussion or argument is likely. Contact key allies prior to the meeting to gain their support for your agenda topic.

Hints

Here are helpful guidelines for agendas:

_____   Always bring additional copies of the agenda to the meeting.

_____   Position important items or action items at the beginning or near the end of an agenda to maintain the interest of participants.

_____   Limit the number of items on the agenda so that meetings are focused.

_____   Label agenda topics (discussion, information, or action) so participants know what is expected.

_____   When distributing the agenda in advance, attach reports, minutes, articles, or executive summaries that relate to topics on the agenda. Any additional information to be distributed at the actual meeting should not exceed one page in length; otherwise, participants will not have time to digest the material.

_____   Review the agenda before the meeting and make notes on the outcomes you wish to achieve. After the meeting, evaluate whether these goals were achieved.

Agenda Ambush?

Nancy is the junior partner in a rapidly growing firm. She has three issues she wants to discuss with senior members. Nancy asks her secretary to set up a convenient meeting time for this group.

Two days later Nancy walks into the meeting and is asked to chair a committee that one of the senior partners will be unable to host. A second senior partner hands her a copy of a speech that she has to present that evening at a fundraiser. A third partner passes along two additional assignments for Nancy to handle as soon as possible.

Finally, Nancy is able to bring up the three issues she feels are important. The senior members reply that they will consider two of them, but that the third is out of the question. They thank Nancy for bringing the matters to their attention, and let her know that they will contact her if they have anything more to say. ∎

4

How could Nancy have arranged the meeting so her agenda would be given more attention?

_____

_____

_____

_____

(See page 51 for a suggested solution.)

Reminder—when constructing agendas, follow the basic rules of written communication.

1. Neatness counts—the agenda, like any other written material, creates an impression of the person who created it.
2. Check grammar, punctuation, and spelling (particularly names).
3. Write in a clear, concise style.
4. Ask a colleague to review your draft and make suggestions for improvement.

Finally, remember that every meeting has at least several agendas—the formal printed agenda that is distributed in advance, and the agendas that others bring to the table for discussion. Balancing the agendas while still working on problem solving is the sign of a skillful meeting leader.

Develop your own agenda for an upcoming meeting, or, if you are not involved in planning an upcoming meeting, critique an existing agenda.

Fill in:

Date _____

Time _____

Location _____

Attendees _____

Time schedule and topics _____

Agenda Maintenance

The policy in Jessica's company is to rotate the responsibility of chairing the annual board meeting. This year is Jessica's turn. She has asked each board member for items to include on the agenda. As she looks over the items, she notices that one member has far more items than anyone else.

Jessica formalizes the final agenda and distributes it two days prior to the actual meeting. The member who forwarded the numerous topics approached Jessica, quite irate that many of his items had been deleted. Jessica privately mentioned that she cut items due to the length of time set for the meeting, not because of the items' level of importance.

On the day of the actual meeting, Jessica noticed the animosity of a few members. Soon after the introductory comments, several board members began informal conversations. Eventually these discussions led away from Jessica's planned agenda. Finally, the board member with the list of topics took charge of the meeting. In doing so, he introduced a number of his own topics that Jessica cut from the agenda. ■

How could Jessica have avoided this feud and kept her agenda on track?

_____
_____
_____
_____

(See page 51 for a suggested solution.)

MEETING PLANS

In the case of multiday meetings, planners often construct a *meeting plan*. A meeting plan is more complicated than an agenda because it is a more detailed outline of the entire meeting. Most often meeting plans are used when meetings are held at off-site facilities. Meeting plans often include:

- Schedule of events (index)—times, dates, locations, and attendees.
- Hotel information—management contacts.
- Budget and insurance information.
- Supplier information—audiovisual equipment, printing, or transportation.
- Food service information—dining room, surcharges, or menus.
- Site inspection checklist.
- Registration information—flights, VIP request, dietary request, or time of arrival.
- Daily plans of each meeting—seating charts, menus, or materials.
- Evaluation instrument.

Hotels or conference centers refer to specification sheets for these meeting plans and use them to provide a comprehensive overview of the entire program for their in-house staff. When you've planned an off-site meeting, consult frequently with the hotel sales and service manager to ensure that the details of the meeting plan match the information on the hotel's specification sheets.

AUDIOVISUAL EQUIPMENT

Most successful meetings incorporate audiovisual (AV) presentations. As a meeting planner, chairperson, or presenter you should be knowledgeable about basic forms of AV, and you should also know when and where to turn for assistance if you need equipment.

When working with a hotel, find out exactly what equipment they have in-house and what must be ordered from outside sources. In addition, ask if there is an on-site service manager available if problems should arise.

Choose the Right Equipment

On this list of commonly used audiovisual equipment, label those items that you think would work best with small (S) meeting groups, with large (L) meeting groups, or with either (E) size group.

_____   Lecterns. These are speaker stands to hold the presenter's notes. Elaborate lecterns have central controls for room lighting, sound, and audiovisual equipment.

4

——————— Screens. Projection screens come in many types. Some are permanently positioned in the wall, others pull down from the ceiling, and portable models have tripods. In addition, screens have different surfaces affecting the degree of brilliance.

——————— Slide Projectors. The 35mm carousel is a standard item. Most slide trays hold 80 2 × 2 inch slides.

——————— Flipcharts, Chalkboards, and Whiteboards. Of these three, flipcharts and their easels are the most portable, while chalkboards and whiteboards are usually permanent wall fixtures in meeting rooms.

——————— VCRs. A few of the more common types of video presentations are motivational tapes, sales training, and staff development. Standard format is VHS half-inch tape.

——————— Microphones. The most basic of all audio equipment, microphones come in various shapes and sizes. Hand, lavaliere, and wireless microphones allow more mobility than stationary desk or lectern microphones.

——————— Overhead Projectors. Relatively simple devices, overheads project images onto a screen or wall surface.

Now, check your answers against the information in the table below.

Equipment	Advantages	Disadvantages
Overhead projectors	Simple to use Inexpensive materials Speaker faces audience Used in lighted room	Distracting fan noise Often illegible material Dull or wordy material Viewed as dated technology

Hints for use
- Limit to groups of 50 participants.
- Do not leave the projector running if not needed—it is very distracting.
- Mount transparencies on cardboard frames for ease of handling.
- Develop professional transparencies (use of computer graphics).
- Mask areas of the transparency not under discussion.
- Use a pointer to indicate items on the screen.
- Give the audience enough time to read the material.
- Limit transparencies to one point, seven lines, and 20 words.

Slide projectors	Strong color image Use of remote control Easy to revise presentation	Distracting fan/slide noise Darkened room Viewed as dated technology

Hints for use
- Do not leave a slide on the screen if you begin a new topic.
- Turn off the light but not the fan immediately after the meeting.
- Limit slides to one point, seven lines, and 20 words.
- Lettering should be large and legible.
- Charts and graphs work better than words only.

Equipment	Advantages	Disadvantages
Flipcharts	Inexpensive Easy to revise Good for brainstorming	For small groups only Often unprofessional Unstable

Hints for use
- Use dark color markers on white paper.
- Print legibly using upper- and lowercase letters.
- Use only with small groups and interactive sessions.
- Leave blank sheets between printing to avoid "bleeding."

Chalkboards/Whiteboards	Readily available Easy to use Easy to revise	Messy Often considered unprofessional Must be erased frequently

Hints for use
- Highlight only key information.
- Write information beforehand to limit having your back to the group.
- Use different colored chalk or markers for variety.

VCRs	Professional image Remote control Lighted room	Equipment complexity Programming complexity Screen size often too small

Hints for use
- Choose screen size using formula of one inch per attendee—use more than one monitor if necessary.
- Arrive early to test tapes, rewind, check sound, and so forth.

The key to using audiovisual equipment effectively is to match the presentation to the audience. Some groups expect professionally prepared videos or computer-generated slides and overheads. Other small, last-minute meetings lend themselves to flipcharts and group interaction. And, of course, budget also influences the type of equipment chosen.

Use the following diagrams to determine where audiovisual equipment (VCR, overhead projector, screen, lectern) should be placed.

PUTTING IT TOGETHER

Each meeting requires specific tools to ensure its success. Some of these tools, such as the agenda, are prepared and distributed ahead of time. Others such as the audiovisual equipment involve careful planning and special arrangements both before and during the meeting.

Planners and chairpersons must be careful to select the appropriate meeting tools to suit the needs of their particular group.

4

a.

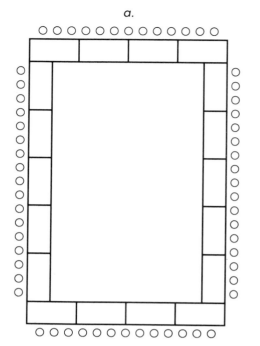

b.

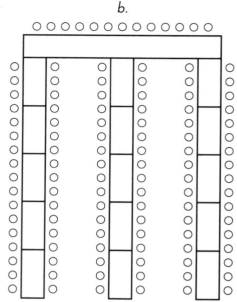

c.

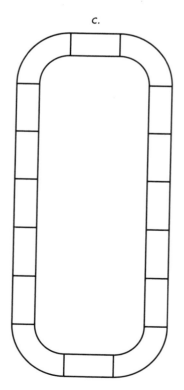

d.

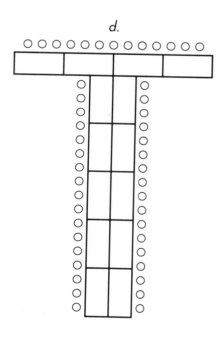

■ Review & Practice

Why should agendas be distributed in advance?

_____

_____

What is the difference between an agenda and a meeting plan?

_____

_____

_____

What audiovisual equipment is most likely to be needed for your next meeting?

_____

_____

_____

4

Chapter Checkpoints

✓ Agendas should be distributed in advance and should be one to two pages in length.

✓ Meeting plans are used for multiday meetings.

✓ Audiovisual equipment contributes to the effectiveness and professionalism of a meeting presentation.

Post-Test

Congratulations! You have just taken another important step in your professional development by completing *Meetings that Work.*

This Post-Test is provided as a means of reinforcing the material you have just covered. If you have difficulty with any question, you can simply refer to the indicated page number for a quick review.

Instructions: Circle the letter of the correct answer.

1. Which of the following are good reasons for holding a meeting?
   a. To exchange information.
   b. To make better decisions.
   c. To delegate tasks or authority.
   d. All of the above.

2. This meeting is primarily motivational and informational. It usually deals with product knowledge, company pride, and marketing issues. What type of meeting is this?
   a. Training.
   b. Sales.
   c. Executive.
   d. Supplier.

3. Look over this list of characteristics: organizational skills, flexibility, listening skills. Decide if they are most important to planners, chairpersons, or attendees.
   a. Planners.
   b. Chairpersons.
   c. Attendees.
   d. All three groups.

4. Nonverbal behavior accounts for _____ percent of communication.

   a. 10.

   b. 25.

   c. 55.

   d. 75.

5. The leader of a meeting should always sit:

   a. Near the middle of the room.

   b. At a corner table.

   c. At the head table or at a podium.

   d. Near the coffee setup.

6. Good listeners often control discussions, yet most people only pay attention to _____ percent of what is said.

   a. 5.

   b. 25.

   c. 50.

   d. 75.

7. Which of the following are unwritten rules?

   a. Never use an official title.

   b. Whoever extends an invitation picks up the check.

8. The following strategies work best when meeting with peers.

   a. Use humor and past experiences, begin formally, refer to higher authority.

   b. Ask for action and commitment, act as a resource.

   c. Outline objectives, seek solutions, delegate.

   d. None of the above.

9. In stage two of teambuilding, leaders should:

   a. Plan, form, and set ground rules.

   b. Organize and form the team.

   c. Lead and move to consensus.

   d. Control and conform.

10. The least important quality of an agenda is:

    a. Focus.

    b. Creativity.

    c. A minimum length of five pages.

    d. Grammar and spelling.

11. The following audiovisual equipment is best used with large groups:

    a. Small VCRs.

    b. Chalkboards.

    c. Flipcharts.

    d. Microphones.

1. **d** 2. **b** 3. **d** 4. **c** 5. **c** 6. **b** 7. **b** 8. **a**
9. **b** 10. **c** 11. **a**

Suggested Solutions

Body Language Speaks a Thousand Words (p. 17)

Jeff has made a number of errors in nonverbal behavior because he did not take his cue from others who had attended previous meetings. The fact that he arrived early and chose a seat near the head of the table indicates his interest, but also indicates that he intends to contribute. He failed to recognize that some seats may be assigned to other attendees. His contributions probably were not significant; therefore at the next meeting that he attends many of his suggestions may be discounted even if they are valid. If anyone saw him doodling rather than taking notes, they will surely assume he is disinterested and inattentive. Apparently, he felt the meeting was not important because he was interrupted for a telephone call and frequently rose to refill his coffee cup. Finally, Jeff may have nothing significant to tell his boss because he may have missed the entire point of the session.

Leadership Styles: Choose One that Works (p. 25)

The purpose of the meetings has changed. Rather than building team spirit, the focus is now on checking details, questioning decisions, and operations. The new manager needs to redirect his actions to build team spirit or work will continue to suffer. Perhaps individual sessions with key participants prior to the weekly meeting would help reach this goal. In addition, the new manager might meet informally with the previous manager. Another strategy might be to ask each member to contribute to the weekly meetings by leading them or organizing them.

Agenda Ambush? (p. 38)

Nancy has forgotten an important rule in meeting planning—everyone comes to the table with his or her own personal agenda. In this case, Nancy is the most junior member present; therefore her bosses will naturally assume that their issues take priority. When dealing with those in higher authority, it may be wise to forward a written agenda prior to the actual meeting and solicit comments. This way unnecessary meetings may be avoided altogether.

If Nancy does not receive feedback, then her course of action is to set forth a written agenda and timetable and forward it one or two days prior to the actual meeting. Finally, Nancy should suggest that the meeting be held in her office. This will set a degree of control and will enable her to set the tone for the meeting.

Agenda Maintenance (p. 40)

In this case, Jessica must deal with a control issue. The member who had numerous meeting items has obviously developed allies to disrupt the meeting so that attention can be focused on his own personal agenda. In doing so, he has destroyed Jessica's credibility. A wiser course of action would have been to make an informal call to this individual to discuss the meeting's time constraints. Jessica could have asked this individual to help her prioritize his concerns so that each attendee would have equal time. The member would have felt that he received personal attention and would have been more sympathetic to Jessica. Perhaps he might have even acted as her ally during the meeting.

Site Selection

As you may know, large-scale meeting planning can be a full-time career. Many large businesses have a department that sets up conferences, functions, and conventions. Employees in this group make sure that all the details that go into planning successful extended meetings are included. Professional meeting planners have close contact with hotel and conference sites, coordinate the various activities during an extended conference, and make critical decisions about appropriate site facilities for particular meetings.

Although you may not have occasion to plan full-scale meetings to the same degree of detail as a meeting planner, you are likely to work with a meeting planner, either within your own company, or when you or your colleagues participate in a conference or meeting sponsored by another organization. This appendix provides a very brief overview of some issues addressed by meeting planners. Keep these in mind the next time you're involved in planning a meeting or working with a meeting planner.

WHERE TO MEET?

In-house or off-site—that is the question that professional meeting planners often ponder when considering the perfect site, because location plays such a key role in the success of meetings.

Routine meetings are most often held in-house in conference rooms, offices, boardrooms, or even cafeterias. Annual sales meetings or other national meetings are usually held off-site at a large hotel or conference area. Professional planners may use a site inspection sheet such as the one on pages 53–56 to evaluate a potential conference location.

Site Inspection Checklist

Property _____

Address _____

Property classification (all-suite, resort, etc.) _____

Location (airport, city center, etc.) _____

(continued)

Site Inspection Checklist

Transportation

Courtesy van _____
Self parking _____
Taxis _____
Transfers _____
Valet parking _____

Facilities

Exterior _____
  Grounds _____
  Maintenance _____
  Noise factors _____
Interior
  Lobby _____
    Airline desks _____
    Bellman _____
    Concierge _____
    Decor _____
    Doorman _____
    Elevators _____
    Lobby bars _____
    Logical floor plan _____
    Luggage storage _____
    Meeting areas _____
    Tour desks _____
  Front desk
    Lines _____
    Staff attitude _____
Rooms
  Types _____
    Singles _____
    Doubles _____
    Twins _____
    Suites _____
  Category
    Standard _____
    Superior _____
    Deluxe _____
  Special features
    Dressing area _____

Site Inspection Checklist

Closet space _____

Bathroom _____

Decor _____

Amenities _____

Lighting _____

Entertainment center _____

View _____

Housekeeping standards _____

Business and meeting facilities

Function rooms _____

Ballroom _____

Break-out space _____

Main meeting room _____

Small conference rooms _____

Audiovisual capacity _____

Services

FAX _____

Copy machine _____

Equipment storage _____

Features

Restaurants

Coffee shop _____

Pool service _____

Room service _____

Full service _____

Lounge/Bar _____

Lobby _____

Poolside _____

Recreation

Beach _____

Golf _____

Health club _____

Shopping _____

Tennis _____

Tour desk _____

Video arcade _____

Nightlife

Disco _____

Nightclub _____

(continued)

Site Inspection Checklist

Booking information
    Special packages _____
        Weekend _____
        Wedding _____
    800 Number _____
    Credit card acceptance _____

Additional notes _____
_____
_____
_____
_____

Meetings Associations

American Hotel & Motel Association
1201 New York Avenue, N.W., Washington, DC 20005
202-289-3100

American Society of Association Executives
1575 I Street, N.W., Washington, DC 20005
202-626-2723

American Society of Travel Agents
1101 King Street Suite 200, Alexandria, VA 22314

Convention Liaison Council
1575 I Street, N.W., Washington, DC 20005
202-626-2764

Exposition Service Contractors Association
1516 S. Pontius Avenue, Los Angeles, CA 90025

International Association of Convention & Visitors Bureaus
1809 Woodfield Drive, Savoy, IL 61874

Meeting Planners International
1950 Stemmons Freeway, Dallas, TX 75207

National Association of Exposition Managers
719 Indiana Ave, Ste. 300, Indianapolis, IN 46202

Professional Convention Management Association
100 Vestavia Office Park, Birmingham, AL 35216

Society of Corporate Meeting Planners
2800 Garden Road, #208, Monterey, CA 93940

Society of Incentive Travel Executives
271 Madison Avenue, New York, NY 10016

Periodicals

Association & Society Manager
Barrington Publications
825 S. Barrington Avenue, Los Angeles, CA 90049

Business Travel News
CMP Publications, Inc.
600 Community Drive, Manhasset, NY 11030

Corporate Meetings & Incentives
Edgell Communications Inc.
7500 Old Oak Boulevard, Cleveland, OH 44130

Corporate Travel
Gralla Publications
1515 Broadway, New York, NY 10036

Incentive Travel Manager
Barrington Publications
825 S. Barrington Avenue, Los Angeles, CA 90049

Meeting News
Gralla Publications
1515 Broadway, New York, NY 10036

Meetings & Conventions
Ziff-Davis Publishing Co.
500 Plaza Drive, Secaucus, NJ 07094

Successful Meetings
Bill Communications
633 Third Avenue, New York, NY 10017

Meetings & Incentive Travel
Southam Communications, Ltd.
1450 Don Mills Road, Ontario M3B2X7

Resorts & Incentives
Gralla Publications
1515 Broadway, New York, NY 10036

The Meeting Manager
Meeting Planners International
1950 Stemmons Freeway, Dallas, TX 75207

Tour & Travel News
CMP Publications, Inc.
600 Community Drive, Manhasset, NY 11030

THE BUSINESS SKILLS EXPRESS SERIES

This growing series of books addresses a broad range of key business skills and topics to meet the needs of employees, human resource departments, and training consultants.

To obtain information about these and other Business Skills Express books, please call Business One IRWIN toll free at: 1-800-634-3966.

Effective Performance Management	ISBN	1-55623-867-3
Hiring the Best	ISBN	1-55623-865-7
Writing that Works	ISBN	1-55623-856-8
Customer Service Excellence	ISBN	1-55623-969-6
Writing for Business Results	ISBN	1-55623-854-1
Powerful Presentation Skills	ISBN	1-55623-870-3
Meetings that Work	ISBN	1-55623-866-5
Effective Teamwork	ISBN	1-55623-880-0
Time Management	ISBN	1-55623-888-6
Assertiveness Skills	ISBN	1-55623-857-6
Motivation at Work	ISBN	1-55623-868-1
Overcoming Anxiety at Work	ISBN	1-55623-869-X
Positive Politics at Work	ISBN	1-55623-879-7
Telephone Skills at Work	ISBN	1-55623-858-4
Managing Conflict at Work	ISBN	1-55623-890-8
The New Supervisor: Skills for Success	ISBN	1-55623-762-6
The *Americans with Disabilities Act:* What Supervisors Need to Know	ISBN	1-55623-889-4